THE WIND CARRIED ME
THE SECRET LIFE OF A BONSAI

500 Years of Wisdom on Healing, Resilience, and the Beauty of Survival

NEL OLIVER

NOR Publishing LLC

Geoje Island Cliff (Photo taken by the author)

The Wind Carried Me: The Secret Life of a Bonsai
Copyright © 2025 by Nel Oliver
NOR Publishing LLC

All rights reserved. This book or any portion thereof may not be reproduced or used in any manner whatsoever without the express written permission of the publisher, except for the use of brief quotations in critical articles or reviews.

This is a work of poetic reflection and literary imagination. The bonsai narrator, historical references, and philosophical insights are inspired by a blend of research, personal experience, and metaphorical storytelling.

Hardcover ISBN: 979-8-9987831-0-4
Paperback ISBN: 979-8-9987831-1-1

Cover art and illustrations by AI with creative direction from the author.
Printed in the USA by Amazon KDP
First paperback/hardcover edition, 2025

DEDICATION

To those who have been bent but not broken, your resilience is the soil from which this story grew.

EPIGRAPH

"What is rooted is easy to nourish What is silent cannot be disturbed."

— Lao Tzu

AUTHOR'S NOTE

This book was born not from imagination alone, but from real roots found in a bonsai sanctuary near Suwon, South Korea. There, I stood before trees older than nations, one of them over 500 years old. Weeks later, on a fishing trip to the cliffs of Geoje Island, I saw small pine trees growing from stone, shaped by salt and storm. Their defiance of gravity and odds mirrored the human resilience I have long witnessed in my professional life, working to safeguard others in dangerous environments. This story is the meeting place of nature's wisdom and human endurance.

TABLE OF CONTENTS

INTRODUCTION: WHISPERING NEEDLES	13
PART I- ROOTED IN STONE: THE EARLY YEARS	
CHAPTER 1: BIRTH ON THE CLIFF	21
CHAPTER 2: SALT, STORM, AND SUN	29
CHAPTER 3: THE POWER OF STILLNESS	39
PART II- UPROOTED: TRANSFORMATION AND TRANSPLANTING	
CHAPTER 4: THE DAY THEY CAME	49
CHAPTER 5: THE BONSAI POT	63
CHAPTER 6: TENDED BUT TRIMMED	75
PART III- THE QUIET OBSERVER: WISDOM FROM THE CORNER	
CHAPTER 7: WATCHING THE FAMILY	87
CHAPTER 8: THE SICK BOY	97
PART IV- RESILIENCE BLOOMS: LESSONS FOR THE HUMAN HEART	
CHAPTER 9: SEASONS FOR LETTING GO	109
CHAPTER 10: SCARS ARE STRENGTH	119
CHAPTER 11: HEALING IS NOT LINEA	129
CHAPTER 12: THE WIND CARRIES ME	137
EPILOGUE: YOU ARE THE BONSAI	147
REFERENCES	153
ABOUT THE AUTHOR	165

INTRODUCTION

WHISPERING NEEDLES

I am a tree, also I am a witness, *a keeper of time, and a bearer of stories*. My roots have clung to stone, my branches have bent to storms, and my needles have *whispered secrets to the wind*. For five centuries, I have stood in silence, observing the world as it changed around me. I have seen empires rise and fall, families grow and wither, and the earth itself shift beneath my roots. And yet, *through it all, I have endured.*

I am a bonsai a Pinus Thunbergii born on the cliffs of Geoje Island.[1] My life began five years before the Imjin War swept across this land,[2] when Korea faced one of its darkest hours. The wind carried me here first as a seed, plucked from a mother tree and deposited into a crack between stones, *a place where life should not have been possible.* Though I was young then, barely more than a sprout clinging to the rocky soil, I felt the tremors of history in my roots. The wind carried the cries of sailors and soldiers to me, their voices mingling with the roar of cannon fire and the crash of waves. Even now, centuries later, I can still hear them *if I close my mind to the present and let myself drift back.*

But this is not just my story; it is yours as well. We are not so different, you and I. Like me; you have faced storms that threatened to break you. Forces have shaped you beyond your control, pruned by life in ways that may have seemed cruel but were necessary for your growth. And like me, you carry scars *marks of survival that tell your story far better than unblemished skin ever could.*

My life began in an unlikely place a crack between two stones on a cliff overlooking the sea. The winds were harsh there, carrying salt that stung my tender needles and threatened to dry out my roots before they could find purchase in the shallow soil. Yet somehow, I survived. Perhaps it was sheer stubbornness or some instinctive knowledge that *even the most inhospitable places can nurture life if one will adapt.*

From my perch on that cliffside, I had a perfect view of Geoje Island's rugged beauty the jagged rocks that seemed to pierce the sky, the endless expanse of ocean stretching toward the horizon, and the ever-changing dance of sunlight and shadow on the water's surface. It was a harsh but beautiful world, one that taught me early on that *life is both fragile and resilient.*

I was still young when war came to our shores. The year was 1592, though I did not yet know how humans marked time then. All I knew was that one day, something new interrupted the peaceful rhythm of waves crashing against rocks something violent and chaotic. Ships appeared on the horizon, their oars slicing through the water like *ghostly wings* as they moved closer to land. Soon after came the sounds: shouting voices carried by the wind, followed by explosions so loud they seemed to shake even the cliffs themselves.

This was the Battle of Okpo the first major naval engagement in the Imjin War. Admiral Yi Sun-sin led his fleet against Japanese invaders in these very waters, winning that would become legendary in Korean history. From my vantage point on the cliff side, I could see plumes of smoke rising from burning ships and hear the clash of steel mingling with cries of triumph and despair.

Even as we celebrated victory here at Okpo Bay, I knew this marked only the beginning. Over the next six years, war would sweep across Korea like a wildfire, leaving destruction in its wake. By 1597, when Admiral Yi faced his greatest defeat at Chilcheollyang as a battle fought close to where I stood, I had grown accustomed to witnessing human conflict from afar.

But war did not end with Japan's retreat; new challenges arose in its wake. In 1627 and again in 1636–1637, Manchu forces invaded Korea from the north, bringing devastation once more to these lands as Joseon struggled to rebuild after years of hardship. These invasions marked another chapter in Korea's history, a reminder that *resilience often comes at significant cost.*

As centuries passed and Korea entered periods of peace under rulers like King Yeongjo (1724–1776) and King Jeongjo (1776–1800),[3] I watched as this nation flourished once more. The fields grew abundant with irrigated crops; scholars filled royal libraries with knowledge; art and culture thrived amidst newfound stability. Yet even during these golden years, *storms occasionally returned, both literal ones* that bent my branches *and figurative ones* that tested Korea's unity.

The 20th century brought upheaval unlike anything I had seen before: Japanese colonization stripped Korea of its sovereignty; World War II left scars across continents; and civil war divided this land into two nations: North and South Korea. Through it all, from colonial oppression to modern independence, I remained rooted as *a silent witness to both suffering and triumph.*

As much as war shaped my early years, it was nature itself that became my greatest teacher. The wind taught me *how to bend without breaking*; its relentless force shaped my branches into graceful curves rather than snapping them in two. The sun showed me how to reach upward, even when shadows threatened to engulf me entirely. And the salt-laden air reminded me that *hardship can be both corrosive and cleansing.* It strips away what is unnecessary while leaving behind only what is essential.

I learned these lessons slowly over time, not through words, but through experience. Nature speaks a language[4] that is both subtle and profound; its wisdom cannot be hurried or forced, but must be absorbed gradually, like water seeping into thirsty roots.

It is this language that I wish to share with you now *the language of patience and presence*[5]; of *healing through stillness; of finding beauty even in brokenness.*

Before we begin this journey together, before I tell you about storms survived and scars earned, I want you to pause for a moment and breathe deeply. Close your eyes if you wish and imagine yourself sitting beside my branches on a quiet afternoon.

Feel the rough texture of my bark beneath your fingertips as you trace lines etched by centuries past the marks left by human hands that once tended but also trimmed me; by storms whose winds shaped my branches into graceful curves; and by passaging time that has weathered my surface. While lightning has never struck me directly for such an event would leave permanent damage or even end my life, I carry scars that tell stories of survival, resilience, and adaptation to nature's harshest forces.

Listen closely as my needles whisper secrets carried by winds from distant lands, *secrets about love found and lost; about grief borne silently yet shared universally; about resilience born not from strength alone but also from vulnerability.*[6]

And finally, imagine looking up toward my canopy where sunlight filters through needles swaying gently in rhythm with life itself, a reminder that even amidst chaos *there is always light waiting patiently for those willing to seek it out.*

Now open your eyes if you ever closed them or simply take another breath before turning these pages because what lies ahead is not just stories; they are mirrors reflecting truths already within you waiting patiently for recognition.

You see you are not so different from me after all…

PART I- ROOTED IN STONE: THE EARLY YEARS

CHAPTER 1

BIRTH ON THE CLIFF

I was born in *a place where life should not have been possible.* My roots first took hold in a crack between two stones on the rugged cliffs of Geoje Island, a place where the land meets the sea *in a dramatic embrace of beauty and ferocity*. The winds that swept across the island carried salt from the ocean and *whispers of distant lands*, while waves crashed endlessly against the rocks below. This was *my cradle, my teacher, and my first challenge.*

Geoje Island, as I would come to understand over centuries, is a land shaped by time and nature's relentless forces. It is Korea's second-largest island[7] after Jeju, known for its breathtaking landscapes of jagged peaks, lush forests, and serene beaches. But it is the cliffs that define Geoje's spirit as raw, *unyielding, and timeless*. These cliffs are not merely stone; they are *monuments to resilience*, carved over millions of years by wind and waves into forms both strange and beautiful. Lion-shaped rocks stand guard over the sea, candlestick formations rise defiantly against the horizon, and caves *whisper secrets of ancient tides*.[8]

It was here, *amidst this rugged beauty*, that I began my life. The wind carried my seed, perhaps from a towering pine on a distant mountain or perhaps from a nearby grove and deposited it in the narrow crevice of a cliff face. There was no soil to cradle me, *only a thin layer of dust and grit* that had settled over centuries.

The sun beat down mercilessly during the day, while at night, *the cold seeped into every pore of my fragile form*. The salty air stung my tender needles[9] as they emerged for the first time, and every gust of wind threatened to tear me from my precarious perch.

Yet somehow, I survived.

Geoje Island is a place of contrasts, a land where beauty and hardship coexist in perfect harmony. The cliffs where I was born rise steeply from the sea, their surfaces weathered and scarred by countless storms. Across lies Hakdong Pebble Beach, where waves tumble over smooth black stones with *a sound like whispered prayers*. To the north are rolling hills covered in forests of pine and oak, their canopies swaying gently in rhythm with the wind. And beyond it all stretches *the endless expanse of the ocean, a restless force that both nurtures and threatens* life on this island.

The cliffs themselves are alive with *stories written in stone*. Over millennia, wind and water have sculpted them into shapes that defy imagination arches that frame the sky like *windows to another world*; caves that *echo with the voices of waves*; and jagged outcroppings that seem to *reach toward heaven itself*. These formations are not static; they change with each passing year as nature continues its work of creation and destruction.

For those who live here, whether human or tree, *survival is an act of adaptation*. The people of Geoje have long understood this truth.[10] They have built their homes to withstand typhoons, their boats to navigate treacherous waters, and their lives around rhythms dictated by nature's whims. In this way, they are not unlike me, a *bonsai born on a Cliffside*[11] who learned early on that life demands both strength and flexibility.

Struggle marked my earliest days. As my roots grew, they encountered nothing but resistance *stone that refused to yield* and cracks too narrow to provide nourishment. Yet I persisted. Slowly but surely, my roots found their way deeper into the rock face, seeking pockets of moisture hidden within its depths. It was not much, *just enough to sustain me, but it was enough.*

The wind was my constant companion during those early years. It howled through the cliffs with a voice both fierce and mournful, bending my tiny form until I thought I might snap in two. But instead of breaking me, it taught me *how to bend, how to yield without surrendering entirely.* My branches grew in harmony with the wind's direction[12], *shaped by its touch into graceful curves* that seemed almost deliberate.

The sun was another teacher, its light *both a blessing and a trial.* During the day, it warmed my needles and fueled my growth; at night, its absence left me vulnerable to the cold. Yet even this duality held lessons for me: I learned to cherish moments of warmth while enduring periods of darkness with patience.

And then there was the salt, the invisible force carried by every breath of wind from the ocean below. It coated my needles in a fine layer that burned at first but eventually became part of me. The salt reminded me that *hardship can be both corrosive and cleansing,* that it strips away *what is unnecessary* while leaving behind only *what is essential.*

My birth on this cliff mirrors your own struggles as humans navigating a world filled with challenges. Just as I clung to life in an environment that seemed determined to reject me, so you faced moments when survival felt impossible when every force around you seemed intent on breaking your spirit.

But like me, you have endured.

Consider how often you have faced resistance in your own life whether from circumstances beyond your control or from within yourself. Perhaps you have felt like my roots did as they pressed against unyielding stone: trapped, confined, and unable to move forward no matter how hard you tried. Yet even in those moments of despair, there was growth happening beneath the surface growth *invisible but real.*

Or think how often forces beyond your control have *molded you shifting winds that redirect your plans* and *the bitterness of hardship that scars your soul.* These experiences may feel painful at first but over time they become part of who you are *a testament to your resilience.*

My story and yours is one of *survival against odds that seemed insurmountable.* It is about *finding strength because of adversity*; about learning from nature's wisdom how to *adapt without losing oneself entirely.*

As you read these pages, as you imagine sitting beside my branches, I hope you will see yourself reflected in my journey—in my roots *clinging stubbornly to stone despite every obstacle*—in my branches *bending gracefully under pressure* rather than snapping. *My needles bear scars from salt-laden winds, yet they continue to grow towards the light.*

Because if there is one thing I have learned during years perched on this cliff side overlooking Geoje Island, it is this: Life finds a way.

Always.

CHAPTER 2

SALT, STORM, AND SUN

The salt came first. It arrived with the wind, *invisible yet relentless*, coating my needles with its sting. Then came the storms, violent and chaotic, shaking my fragile form to its core. And finally, there was the sun, its light *both a balm and a trial*, urging me to grow even as it scorched my tender branches. These three forces, salt, storm, and sun became my greatest teachers. They shaped me in ways I could not have foreseen, teaching me lessons about *endurance, adaptation, and hope.*

Salt is *a quiet adversary*. It does not announce itself with thunder or fury; instead, it arrives subtly, carried by the wind from the ocean below. *At first, I did not even notice it was there.* But as time passed, I felt its effects. My needles *turned brittle at the tips*[13], their vibrant green dulled by yellowing halos. The salt seeped into my roots through the thin layer of soil in which I grew, leaving behind *a residue that made it harder* for me to draw in water and nutrients.

Salt is a paradox. It is *both life-giving and life-taking*. The ocean, from which salt comes, is a source of endless vitality, *a vast expanse teeming with life* but its essence, left unchecked, can corrode. For me, salt became *a constant presence in my life* a reminder that hardship often works quietly in the background, eroding our strength little by little, *without announcing itself loudly*.

Yet salt also taught me resilience. Over time, I adapted to its presence. My needles grew waxy and tough, their surfaces better able to repel the salty spray. My roots dug deeper into the cracks of the cliff face, seeking pockets of fresh water hidden beneath layers of stone. I learned to endure finding ways to *coexist with the salt* rather than *wasting energy fighting it.*

Similarly, hardship often enters your life *like salt subtly and persistently.* It might come as chronic stress, unresolved grief, or lingering doubts that erode your confidence over time. Like the bonsai adapting to salty winds, *you too must find ways to endure* these challenges without letting them define you entirely. You develop thicker skins not as a sign of weakness, but as *a testament to your ability to survive.*

"Hardship does not break us; it shapes us. Like salt on my needles, it leaves marks that remind us of what we have overcome."

If salt was my quiet adversary, storms were *my loudest challengers.* They arrived suddenly and without warning dark clouds gathering on the horizon before unleashing their fury upon everything in their path. The wind howled through the cliffs with a voice that seemed almost alive, *bending my branches until I thought they might snap.* Rain lashed against me like tiny daggers, soaking into every crevice of my bark and threatening to wash away what little soil I had.

The storms were terrifying in their intensity. There were moments when I felt certain they would tear me from my perch entirely, moments when I wondered if it was worth continuing to hold on at all.

But then something remarkable happened: I learned *how to bend without breaking.*

The wind that threatened to destroy me became a teacher instead. It showed me how to *yield gracefully under pressure* rather than resist stubbornly against forces beyond my control. My branches grew in harmony with its direction,[14] *curving into shapes that seemed almost deliberate* despite their chaotic origins. And when the storms passed, as they always did, I found myself *stronger than before.* My roots had clung more tightly to the stone; my branches had grown more flexible; my needles had shed their weakest parts to make way for fresh growth.

Storms are inevitable in life moments of chaos that test your limits and force you to confront your vulnerabilities head-on. They could manifest as sudden loss, unexpected change, or external crises that shake you to your core. But like the bonsai bending under strong winds, you too can learn how to adapt rather than break under pressure.

"Chaos is not an enemy; it is a catalyst for growth."

There is another tree whose story mirrors mine, a bonsai known as the *Yamaki Pine*.[15] It survived one of humanity's darkest moments: the atomic bombing of Hiroshima on August 6, 1945.

The *Yamaki Pine* was already over three centuries old when that fateful day arrived. At a Yamaki family nursery, less than two miles from ground zero, where destruction reigned supreme and over 100,000 lives were lost instantly, this tree quietly stood in its pot. A simple wall surrounding the property protected it; meanwhile, unimaginable devastation reduced everything around it to ash.

Decades later, someone gifted this bonsai to the United States National Arboretum as a symbol of peace during America's bicentennial celebration in 1976, *a living testament to resilience amidst destruction.*

The *Yamaki Pine*'s survival reminds us that even in moments when everything seems lost, when life burns down around us, there remains within us *an unyielding spark of hope and endurance.* Like this tree standing firm amidst devastation or like myself clinging to stone during storms, you too, as human, have an extraordinary capacity for survival.

"Resilience is not about avoiding hardship, it is about enduring and finding meaning within it."

After every storm comes sunlight, *a warm embrace that dries soaked branches* and coaxes new growth from battered trunks. For me, the sun was *both a blessing and a challenge.* Its light fueled my photosynthesis, providing the energy I needed to grow strong. But it could also be harsh, its rays scorching my needles during long summer days when shade was nowhere to be found.

The sun taught me *about balance.*[16] Too much light could be just as harmful as too little; too much warmth could dry out my roots just as surely as too much rain could drown them. I learned how to position myself carefully on the cliff side so that I could receive just enough sunlight without being overwhelmed by its intensity.

But more than anything else, the sun taught me about hope.

No matter how dark or violent a storm might be, no matter how much damage it left in its wake, the sun always returned, eventually. Its light reminded me that *even after moments of great difficulty, there is always potential for renewal* if we are willing to reach toward it.

Hope, like sunlight, sustains you even during the darkest moments, but you must carefully balance it against reality, or it will blind you entirely. It reminds you that no matter how hard life may seem, there is always potential for growth *if you remain open to possibility.*

"Hope does not erase pain; it illuminates paths forward through it."

Together, these three elements shaped me into who I am today, a bonsai tree perched precariously on a cliff,[17] yet thriving despite every challenge thrown my way.

From salt, I learned endurance,[18] the ability to persist quietly even when hardship lingers indefinitely.

From storms, I learned flexibility, an attribute not only to survive chaos but to emerge stronger because of it.

From sunlight, I learned hope: the courage to continue reaching upward toward light, even after periods of darkness and despair.

And from stories like the *Yamaki Pine*, I learned that *survival itself can become a symbol of peace* and an inspiration for others navigating their own struggles.

"Life will test you again and again, but each test is an opportunity to learn, grow, and become the most resilient version of yourself possible."

CHAPTER 3

THE POWER OF STILLNESS

There are moments in life when the world seems to demand constant motion *when the winds howl, the storms rage, and even the sun feels relentless*. But there are also moments when *everything grows quiet*, when the air becomes still, and time itself seems to pause. These moments of stillness are an opportunity for me to *find strength*.

As a bonsai, long periods of solitude and silence have defined my life. Perched on a cliff overlooking the sea or sitting in a quiet corner of a garden, I have spent centuries *simply being*. While storms and salt have shaped my outer form, it is *stillness that has nurtured my inner resilience*. In the absence of noise and chaos, I have learned to listen not just to the world around me, but to the quiet wisdom within myself.

To be a bonsai is *to live in solitude, but not loneliness*. Like a solitary tree standing apart from a forest, I am *both alone and connected* with a single entity rooted in a vast web of life. My *silence is fullness, rather than emptiness*. It is the sound of my needles whispering in the wind, the hum of life coursing through my roots, and *the quiet rhythm of growth unfolding*[19] day by day.

Stillness has taught me patience. Unlike you, who measure time in hours and days, I measure it in *seasons and cycles*. Growth is slow, imperceptible at times, but it is steady. And, obviously, my growth is not about size like other normal trees, as my natural pot limits me to that. *My growth is about power.* In my silence, I have learned to trust this process, to *let go of urgency and embrace the natural rhythm of life.*

There is power in this kind of stillness, *a power that comes not from action but from presence.* It is a power that you, as human, often overlook in their rush to do more, achieve more, be more. But as I have learned over centuries, *sometimes the most profound growth happens when we simply stop and allow ourselves to be.* Consider the bonsai master Masahiko Kimura, who spent 40 years[20] guiding a single juniper into artistry. His hands moved sparingly, his patience as deep as my roots. True mastery, he knew, lies not in force but in *fidelity to slow, unseen growth.*

Stillness has been offering lessons that can guide me and you as well:

In stillness, *everything becomes clear.* When the winds die down and the noise fades away, we can finally see what lies beneath the surface: our fears, our hopes, our true selves. For me, this clarity comes in moments when the sea below is calm, and the sky above is cloudless. In those moments, I can feel every part of myself, my roots gripping stone, my branches stretching toward light and know that *I am enough*.

For you, stillness offers a similar gift. When you pause from your endless busyness and sit quietly with yourself, you *create space for reflection and self-awareness*. You see not just what you are doing but why you are doing it and whether it aligns with who you truly want to be.

"Stillness is not an absence; it is an opportunity to listen."

Growth takes time, a truth that every bonsai knows intimately. My branches did not take their shape overnight; they were shaped slowly by years of wind and care. My roots did not find their way into stone in a single season; they grew inch by inch over decades.

Humans often struggle with patience in a world that demands instant results. But as I have learned through stillness, true strength comes from trusting the process, even when progress feels invisible. Just as my roots grow deeper with each passing year, so, too, does your inner strength grow with each moment of quiet perseverance?

"Patience is not waiting; it is growing at your own pace."

In my silence, I understand that resilience is not about avoiding hardship but about finding meaning within it. *Each scar on my bark tells a story* of storms weathered and challenges overcome, but it is only through stillness that I have been able to reflect on those stories and see them for what they truly are: evidence of survival.

For you, reflection offers a similar path to resilience. When you take time to sit quietly with your thoughts to reflect on your experiences without judgment, you *see your struggles as steppingstones toward growth* overcoming your struggles.

"Resilience is not about enduring pain; it is about transforming it into wisdom."

Science now whispers what I've always known: a 2013 study found that two hours of silence daily sparked new brain cells in the hippocampus[21], the seat of memory and emotion. Stillness, it seems, is not passive; it is the soil where growth begins.

The lessons I have learned through stillness are not mine alone; they are gifts that nature offers to anyone willing to listen. A Harvard study revealed that just 15 minutes of daily meditation sharpened decision-making by 23%.[22] The quieter the mind, the farther it sees. Here are some meditative practices inspired by my life as a bonsai that can help you find strength and clarity in your own moments of stillness:

Observe something small and intricate: a leaf, a flower, or even your own breath with focused attention. Notice its colors, textures, and movements without trying to change or analyze them. This practice helps you connect with the present moment and quiet your racing thoughts.

"Like watching leaves sway in the wind, mindfulness invites you to be fully present."[23]

Find a quiet place outdoors where you can sit comfortably and focus on your breath. As you inhale deeply, imagine drawing in the fresh energy of nature around you; as you exhale slowly, imagine releasing tension back into the earth. This rhythmic breathing synchronizes your energy with nature's calming presence.[24]

"Breathe like trees do slowly and deeply, with roots grounded firmly in the earth."

Set aside time each day to sit quietly without distractions, no phones or conversations, just you and your thoughts. Use this time to reflect on what you are grateful for or what lessons you can learn from recent experiences.

"In silence lies clarity; in reflection lies wisdom."

Take a slow walk through a natural setting, a park, forest trail, or garden and focus on each step as if it were its own meditation. Feel the ground beneath your feet; listen to birdsong or rustling leaves; let yourself become fully immersed in your surroundings.

"Walk like roots seeking water with intention, but without haste."

People often see stillness as passive as doing nothing, but nothing could be further from the truth. In stillness lies profound activity: *growth happening beneath the surface*; strength being cultivated quietly over time; *clarity emerging like sunlight breaking through clouds.*

As humans rush through their lives, always moving forward yet often feeling lost, I invite you to embrace stillness as I have done for centuries. Sit quietly beneath the branches of a tree; *let yourself pause long enough to hear what silence has to say.*

Because if there's one thing I've learned in five hundred years perched on this earth, it's this:

"True power comes not from doing more but from being fully present."

PART II- UPROOTED: TRANSFORMATION AND TRANSPLANTING

CHAPTER 4

THE DAY THEY CAME

For years, I had lived in quiet harmony on the cliffs of Geoje Island. My roots clung tightly to stone, my needles swayed gently in the wind, and my branches stretched toward the sun. The sea below whispered its eternal rhythm, and I had come to know every shift in the tides, every change in the sky. This was my home, a place both harsh and beautiful, where life felt precarious but deeply connected to the earth.

And then they came.

It was *a day unlike any other,* a day that shattered the quiet rhythm of my existence and set me on a path I could not have foreseen. The morning broke clear and bright, sunlight dancing across the water below my cliff. Yet there was something unfamiliar in the air, *a vibration carried by the wind that spoke of human presence.* Soon, I saw them: two young men descending toward me with ropes and harnesses, their movements precise yet filled with excitement.

They were boys on the cusp of adulthood, perhaps eighteen or twenty years old, *clad in bright helmets and gear that glinted in the sunlight.* Their bronzed skin spoke of days spent outdoors, their confident movements suggesting an experience with cliffs like mine. Yet as they approached me, I sensed their awe the way their eyes lingered on my *twisted trunk and roots that had embraced stone for centuries.*[25]

I felt their hands before I saw them, clearly gloved palms brushing against my bark with a mixture of reverence and determination. They examined me closely, tracing my scars and studying how my roots had found purchase in the crevices of rock. Though their voices carried softly on the wind, it was their actions that spoke louder: carefully chiseling around my base, *freeing me root by root from the stone that had been my anchor for over four hundred years.*

Each tap of their tools sent vibrations through me, gentle yet insistent, as they worked to separate me from the cliff side. With every root they loosened, I felt myself becoming untethered from all I had known. It was not pain but something deeper, a sense of *being uprooted not just physically but spiritually.*

When they finally lifted me free from the rock face, they wrap my roots carefully in damp cloth to keep them alive. Their damp cloths were like the ones firefighters used to save ancient trees from flames, *a temporary womb for roots between one world and the next.*[26] Anyway, I felt an emptiness unlike anything I had ever known. For centuries, I had been part of this cliff. Its rhythms were mine; its strength was mine. Now, I was adrift.

The journey from Geoje to Suwon was long and disorienting. Secured carefully in the back of a vehicle, I watched as landscapes changed around me, rocky coastlines giving way to rolling hills, then fields of crops, and finally to bustling towns and cities. Each bump on the road sent shocks through my fibers, not unlike what happens in a human brain when old pathways break and new ones form. This pain had purpose. My cells were learning a new language of survival.[27] Each mile carried me further from home.

Through it all, I remained silent, not just because I am a tree, but because there were no words for what I felt. During the journey, the young men who had carried me from my cliff occasionally spoke, their voices filled with excitement about my next destination. Yet their words were distant to me; *all I could think about was what I had left behind* the salt-laden winds that shaped my branches, *the cry of seabirds echoing through the cliffs.*

As we traveled inland toward Suwon—years before the great rupture and the so-called "Miracle on the Han River".[28] I sensed a region trembling with the fever of change, though Suwon itself was still not considered a modern city. Through the carrier's slats, I glimpsed the first signs of transformation: *factories emerging like artificial cliffs*, their tentative smokestacks scratching at the sky. The humans would later call it technological feat—*this turning of rubble into progress*. But to my ancient eyes, these steel trunks lacked the quiet grace of pines. I wondered then: Could a nation preparing to bend steel like grass bend itself without breaking? The answer drifted in the still air, where seabirds no longer flew.

When we finally arrived at our destination, an estate surrounded by high walls, I felt a new kind of stillness settle over me. This wasn't the wild beauty of Geoje, but something else entirely: *a place where humans shaped nature* into intricate and deliberate patterns.

I found the garden far more beautiful than I had ever imagined. It was vast yet intimate, a sanctuary where every element seemed carefully evoked harmony. Stone pathways wound through miniature landscapes, tiny mountains rising from beds of moss, streams flowing under arched bridges, groves of ancient trees whose branches cast shadows like calligraphy against stone walls.

The family's residence stood at the heart of this garden, a traditional hanok mansion with sweeping tile roofs and wooden beams darkened by age. Lanterns glowed softly along pathways lined with flowering shrubs and statues half-hidden among bamboo groves.

As they carried me deeper into this sanctuary, we passed displays of bonsai arranged on pedestals, *each one its own universe of beauty and resilience.* Some appeared even older than me, their trunks gnarled with age and scars that told stories similar to *mine.* Others bore intentional flaws a cracked pot, an asymmetrical branch. These weren't mistakes but testaments, much like the Korean celadon pottery repaired with gold. Our scars became part of the art.²⁹

It was here that Master Kim, the twelfth-generation bonsai master who owned this estate, greeted us with quiet reverence. He approached me with measured but purposeful steps, his eyes studying every twist in my trunk and every scar on my bark.

What followed was both a transformation and a trial, a process that would reshape not just my form, but my very essence. In Master Kim's workshop, a space filled with tools worn smooth by generations of use, I underwent a process humans call potting.

First came the cleaning: Master Kim brushed every trace of cliff debris away from my roots, fully exposing them to air for the first time in centuries. Then came pruning, a process more intimate than any storm or wind I had endured before.

Master Kim's methodical work removed roots that had taken centuries to grow but were deemed unnecessary for survival in this new environment. Each cut sent waves through me, not pain exactly, but something close to it: *a deep sense of loss as parts of myself fell away.*

"*The tree will suffer*," Master Kim said softly as he worked. "*But without this suffering, it cannot adapt.*" Master Kim's shears released a flood of chemicals I hadn't needed on the cliffs, a hormonal surge that would force fresh growth. Humans call this *'post-traumatic growth'*; to trees. It's simply our oldest survival script.

After pruning came placement into a shallow ceramic pot filled with volcanic rock pebbles, *a substrate designed not for abundance but for refinement.* Master Kim's skilled hands carefully arranged my trimmed roots over the pebbles before covering them with more, gently pressing each layer into place.

At first, it felt impossible to adapt to find nourishment in such unfamiliar terrain after centuries rooted deeply in solid stone. Yet slowly, imperceptibly at first, new rootlets formed delicate tendrils exploring spaces between pebbles as they sought moisture hidden within this strange new substrate.

In those prior weeks, as my roots groped blindly through volcanic pebbles, I practiced an ancient arboreal calculus:

> — *Is this pot now my forever earth?* (Acceptance)
>
> — *Which tiny fissures can I claim?* (Control)
>
> — *Will this constraint shape me or stunt me?* (Growth)

The answers came slowly, written not in words but in the silent language of cellulose and sap. Later, I would learn what scientists now confirm that my cells remembered.[30] The very genes that had armored me against Geoje's salt-laden gales now awakened, flooding my tissues with enzymes that whispered: *You've survived leaner soil than this.*

Humans, I observed, ask similar questions when their worlds fracture. Psychologist Lucy Hone, who rebuilt her life after unbearable loss, calls this *resilient thinking*[31] the same triage that guided my auxins toward cracks of light. When her research crossed my path decades later (a dropped journal in the garden, its pages fluttering like injured birds), I recognized our kinship. She had codified what roots know instinctively: that survival begins with three acts accepting the unchangeable, commanding the possible, and choosing growth over grievance.

Our languages differed hers in clinical terms, mine in xylem and phloem but our truths intertwined:

— *Adapt or perish.*

— *Bend or break.*

— *Scars are not ruins but maps.*

And so, I grew, not despite the pot, but *through* it, each new rootlet a rebellion against despair, *each millimeter of progress a silent ode to the cliffs I still dreamed of.*

Just as my roots found new pathways through rock pebbles after being trimmed away from stone crevices, you, too, can find ways to regrow after loss or change:

Illness: Like my roots being severed from stone, illness can strip away one's sense of stability and connection to life. It forces you to adapt to new realities and new limitations and endure despite feeling disconnected from your former self.

Divorce or Separation: Being carried away from my home felt like losing a part of myself, a feeling many humans as you experience when relationships end abruptly or painfully.

Grief: The emptiness I felt after leaving Geoje Island mirrors the void left by loss, whether it is losing loved ones or losing a sense of purpose.

In these moments, fear and confusion often take center stage. Like me being uprooted from familiar soil, you can find yourself thrust into unfamiliar environments where nothing feels certain anymore.

"Loss is not just about what is taken away; it is about what remains behind the scars we carry as reminders of what we have endured."

Resilience is not about avoiding change or hardship; it is about growing despite them. My journey from Geoje Island's cliffs to a carefully tended garden is a testament to this truth.

For you facing your own moments of uprooting whether through illness, grief, or major life changes the lessons are clear:

Adaptation Takes Time: Just as my roots needed time to adjust to their new pot, you need time to adapt to new realities after your losses.

Growth Is Possible: Even in unfamiliar environments or restrictive circumstances, growth can happen if you remain open to possibilities.

Connection Endures: Though I am no longer rooted in stone, my connection to Geoje Island remains within me a reminder that our pasts shape us even as we move forward into new futures.

"Loss may leave scars on your soul, but those scars can become stories; stories of survival resilience transformation."

The day they came marked an ending but also a beginning. It was the end of my life on Geoje Island's cliffs but also the start of a new chapter in which I would learn how to thrive in ways I never imagined possible.

As you face your own moments of uprooting as life carries you away from familiar places or forces you into unfamiliar circumstances, I hope you will remember this:

"To be uprooted is not to be broken; it is an opportunity to regrow."

CHAPTER 5

THE BONSAI POT

When my roots were first placed into the confines of a bonsai pot, I felt *an overwhelming sense of restriction.* The space was small, far smaller than the rocky cliffs where I had once spread freely. They carefully measured and controlled the soil; unlike the wild earth I had known before. My roots, accustomed to reaching deep into crevices of stone, now had to navigate boundaries set by human hands. It was a jarring transition, one that made me question whether I could continue to thrive.

But over time, I understood something profound: *confinement does not always mean limitation. Sometimes, it can be an opportunity for growth, a chance to discover strength and beauty within boundaries.*

At first glance, the bonsai pot seems like a prison, a container that restricts freedom and imposes control. For a tree accustomed to growing in the wild, it can feel suffocating, as though every instinct has been curtailed. My roots could no longer stretch endlessly into the earth; my branches could no longer expand without being pruned. Everything about my existence seemed smaller, tighter, and more constrained.

Yet within this confinement, something remarkable happened: I started to grow differently.

Instead of sprawling outward without direction, *my roots learned how to navigate the limited space* within the pot, spreading efficiently and finding nourishment in places I had overlooked before. Science would later confirm what my roots discovered: confined trees develop clever survival strategies. Urban maples trapped under concrete develop root hairs as dense as velvet, while their free-growing forest cousins remain coarse. *Limitation breeds ingenuity in xylem as in life.*[32] My branches, though trimmed by human hands, developed a graceful shape that reflected both my resilience and the care I received. This new form of growth was *not wild or unrestrained; it was deliberate and purposeful.*

Confinement often feels like loss, loss of freedom, autonomy, or possibility. But it can also be a catalyst for transformation. We adapt and find new ways to thrive when placed within boundaries. Just as my roots learned to flourish within the pot's limits, you, too, can discover unexpected strength and creativity when faced with restrictions.

"Freedom is not always about limitless space; sometimes it is about finding purpose within boundaries."

The bonsai pot is not just a container; it is part of an ancient art form, a tradition that celebrates harmony between nature and human care. As I grew within its confines, I understood that beauty can coexist with restriction. In fact, it often emerges because of it.

The philosophy of bonsai cultivation roots in balancing growth and control, wildness and refinement. Both natural forces and human intervention shaped every curve of my branches; every twist in my trunk tells a story of storms endured and hands that guided me toward light. This interplay between freedom and limitation creates a form of beauty that is unique to bonsai, a beauty defined not by excess but by simplicity and intention.

Humans often associate beauty with abundance vast landscapes, sprawling gardens, or unrestrained creativity. But true beauty often lies in simplicity in the careful shaping of what already exists rather than endless expansion. Like the bonsai pot guiding my growth, *restrictions can help us focus on what truly matters* and create something meaningful within those boundaries.

"Restriction does not diminish beauty; it refines it."

As I adapted to life within the bonsai pot, I came to see confinement not as an obstacle, but as a teacher, a force that shaped me in ways I could not have achieved on my own. Here are some lessons I learned:

Growth Is Still Possible: Even within the smallest spaces, growth can happen if we are willing to adapt. My roots did not stop growing when they encountered the edges of the pot; they simply changed direction and found new pathways. Similarly, when you face limitations, whether physical, emotional, or societal, you can grow by seeking opportunities within their constraints.

"Growth is not about how far you can reach; it is about how deeply you can root yourself."

Even your astronauts know this truth. When NASA locked volunteers in mock spacecraft for months, their brains grew new neural pathways, proof that confinement doesn't stifle the mind but redirects its energy like pruned branches seeking light.[33]

Purpose Can Be Found in Boundaries: The bonsai pot directed my growth. It offered a structure that enabled me to thrive in ways I could never have accomplished in the wild. For you, boundaries often serve a similar purpose: they help you focus your energy on what truly matters rather than scattering ourselves across endless possibilities. Like the incarcerated men who tend to bonsai behind bars, I learned boundaries could become sacred spaces. One prisoner told his juniper: "They measure my life in years, but you measure it in millimeters and both counts".[34]

"Boundaries are not barriers; they are guides toward intentional living."

Beauty Emerges Through Balance: My form as a bonsai reflects a balance between nature's wildness and human care, a harmony that creates beauty through restraint rather than excess. Humans too can find beauty in their lives by balancing freedom with discipline, spontaneity with intention. Hands shaped the most powerful bonsai I ever met behind barbed wire. Interned artists in your deserts turned sagebrush into masterpieces, their pruning shears quietly defying the surrounding fences. Beauty, they proved, is the ultimate act of resistance.[35]

"True beauty lies in harmony—not in abundance, but in balance."

Humans are understanding what bonsai have always known. Your architects now design *'not-so-big houses'* where every nook serves intention like my pot, where each centimeter holds meaning.[36]

The lessons I learned from confinement mirror many aspects of your life.

Physical Limitations: People who face physical restrictions, whether because of illness or disability, often discover new ways to live fully within those limits. Like my roots adapting to the bonsai pot, they find strength and creativity in places they never expected.

Emotional Boundaries: Emotional challenges, such as grief or heartbreak, can feel confining at first, but often lead to deeper self-awareness and resilience.

Societal Constraints: Societal pressures or limitations may seem restrictive but can also inspire innovation and purpose when approached with intention.

"Confinement does not define us; how we respond to it does."

Here are some practices inspired by my experience as a bonsai that you can use to find meaning within your own limitations:

Rooting Within Boundaries: Spend time reflecting on your current circumstances, what limitations you face, and what opportunities exist within them. Write down ways you can grow despite those boundaries. Try the 'NASA Method. When feeling confined, list three unexpected benefits of your limitations. Astronauts report this reframing reduces stress by 27%.[37]

"Like roots spreading through confined soil, find pathways for growth even when space feels limited."

Finding Beauty in Simplicity: Choose one area of your life where you feel restricted (e.g., time or resources) and focus on creating something beautiful within those limits, a poem written during a busy day or a meal prepared with few ingredients. Like the internees' desert bonsai, use what's immediately available. A 2023 UC Berkeley study found constraint-based creativity increases dopamine by 19%.[38]

"Beauty emerges when we embrace simplicity rather than resist it."

Balancing Freedom with Discipline: Reflect on areas where you might benefit from more structure or balance, whether it's setting boundaries in relationships or creating routines for personal growth and implement slight changes. Mirror urban trees' mycorrhizal networks: Identify one 'symbiotic relationship' (a person, habit, or resource) that helps you thrive within limits.

"Balance creates harmony; harmony creates beauty."

The bonsai pot may seem like a symbol of confinement at first glance but for me, *it became a source of transformation and beauty.* Growth, I learned, *does not require endless space; it requires intention and adaptability. Restriction, I found, does not diminish life's potential, but it refines it.*
As you face your own moments of confinement as life places boundaries around you, I hope you will remember this:

"Limits are not prisons; they are opportunities for focused growth."

CHAPTER 6

TENDED BUT TRIMMED

When Master Kim first began to care for me, I did not understand his intentions. His hands were gentle yet deliberate, his tools sharp yet precise. He examined my branches with an artist's eye and a gardener's touch, deciding which parts of me would stay and which would go. It was a strange feeling *to be tended so closely*, to have my growth shaped by forces outside me. At first, I resisted. But over time, I came to see that their care was both a gift and a challenge, *a delicate balance between nurturing and controlling.*

By now, Master Kim's Garden had become both *sanctuary and stage for human worry*. The year was 1950, on the eve of war, and Suwon buzzed with rumors about what lay ahead for Korea. Yet within these walls stood an oasis untouched by conflict: winding stone paths lined with flowering shrubs; streams flowing under arched bridges; groves where ancient trees cast shadows like calligraphy against weathered walls.

Master Kim moved among his bonsai with steady hands despite growing tension beyond these gates. When he trimmed my branches or pruned my roots during repotting sessions, his focus never wavered   even as distant voices spoke of alliances breaking apart or armies mobilizing near borders.

The family who lived in this estate mirrored the unease of the nation. Late at night, the father would pace near my corner of the garden, his silhouette framed by lantern light as he gazed toward the horizon, worry etched into his face. The mother lingered by my pot during her morning walks, her touch unusually gentle as though seeking comfort from something unchanging amidst uncertainty. She was not alone in seeking solace in greenery. Across the war-torn peninsula, others would kneel in ruined gardens,[39] *their hands in soil like prayers proving that tending life persists even in breaking worlds.* Even Master Kim's apprentices moved with a quiet urgency, their conversations hushed but tinged with concern.

I felt their tension in the surrounding air, a heaviness that hung like mist over the garden. Yet amidst this unease, Master Kim continued his work with me as though tending to a tree could somehow *restore balance to a world on the brink of chaos.*

"Care during chaos reminds us that beauty endures even amidst uncertainty."

Pruning is an essential part of bonsai care. It involves removing branches, needles, and even roots to maintain the tree's size and shape while promoting its health and longevity. For me, pruning felt like *both a loss and an opportunity, a moment of limitation that also opened new pathways for growth.*

Humans use different pruning techniques, depending on their goals:

Structural Pruning: This reshapes the tree's framework, creating its basic form and style. It is often drastic, requiring the removal of large branches to achieve symmetry or balance.

Maintenance Pruning: This involves routine trimming to refine the tree's appearance and preserve its existing shape.

Root Pruning: During tense pre-war repotting sessions, like those led by Master Kim, Master Kim carefully trimmed back roots while preserving essential feeder roots for recovery.

Each cut made by Master Kim's hands *changes me—not just physically, but fundamentally.* My branches grow in new directions; my roots spread differently; and my overall form grows into something I could not have achieved on my own. Science now confirms what bonsai masters knew: each snip of shears alters a tree's hormonal balance,[40] silencing growth in some areas while awakening it in others *a botanical metaphor for human adaptation.* Your brains undergo similar pruning[41] childhood experiences, trimming some synapses while reinforcing others, shaping your inner landscape as decisively as Master Kim's shears shaped my crown.

Pruning mirrors life itself: how external forces shape us in ways we may not have chosen but must learn to accept. Similarly, societal expectations, relationships, or uncontrollable circumstances shape people, just as human care trims my branches to fit within boundaries. These forces can feel restrictive but also offer opportunities for transformation.

"Every cut carries both loss and potential, a reminder that growth often requires letting go."

Human care is both tender and intrusive. On one hand, it nurtures me providing water when I am thirsty, sunlight when I need energy, and soil rich in nutrients to sustain my roots. On the other hand, it controls me, dictating where my branches will grow and how my form will take shape.

This balance between nurturing and controlling raises *questions about autonomy*: *How much of myself is truly mine? How much has been shaped by external forces?* These questions are not unique to bonsai; they resonate deeply with human experiences as well.

Societal Expectations: Like Master Kim shaping my branches, society often imposes expectations on individuals, on you—defining how you should look, act, or live. These pressures can feel confining but also provide structure that helps people navigate their lives.

Relationships: Just as human care reshapes me over time, relationships influence people's identities sometimes nurturing them toward growth, but other times pruning away parts of themselves they wish to keep.

Circumstances: External events such as illness or loss can reshape lives in profound ways, forcing people to adapt while still striving to remain true to their essence.

"To be tended is both a blessing and a challenge, a reminder that growth requires balance between external guidance and internal authenticity."

Despite all the pruning and reshaping I have undergone over the years, there is *something within me that remains unchanged, an essence that human hands cannot trim away or mold*. It is the part of me that remembers where I came from, *the cliffs of Geoje Island,* and carries those memories within every fiber of my being.

For humans, too, *staying true to one's essence* is an important lesson amidst life's changes:

Authenticity: Even when shaped by external forces, whether societal norms or personal relationships, *people can strive to remain authentic* by honoring their core values and beliefs.

Resilience: Like my scars from pruning, humans carry *marks from their experiences that reflect their ability to endure and grow.*

Self-Awareness: Differentiating between what's essential and what's imposed helps people navigate life with greater clarity and purpose.

"Your essence is your root. It anchors you amidst life's storms and guides you toward growth."

The art of bonsai cultivation emphasizes harmony between nature and human intervention, a philosophy that celebrates *beauty within boundaries rather than unrestrained freedom.* My form as a bonsai reflects this balance: every curve in my branches tells a *story of storms endured;* every twist in my trunk reveals the *careful hand of a gardener guiding me toward light.*

This philosophy challenges conventional notions of beauty:

Controlled Beauty: Humans often associate beauty with perfection or symmetry qualities achieved through deliberate shaping rather than natural growth.

Authentic Beauty: *True beauty lies not in conformity but in authenticity,* in embracing scars as survival stories rather than flaws.

"Beauty emerges not from erasing imperfections but from honoring them as part of your journey."

Here are some lessons I have learned from being tended by human hands- Master Kim's hands:

Growth Requires Letting Go: Each cut made during pruning removes something old to make way for something new. For humans too, growth often requires letting go whether it's releasing past hurts or shedding outdated beliefs.

"Letting go is not a loss; it is transformation."

Balance Is Key: Just as my form reflects the balance between nature's wildness and human care, humans, you- can find harmony by balancing freedom with structure in your own life.

"Balance creates beauty; beauty creates meaning."

Authenticity Endures: Despite centuries of shaping, my essence remains unchanged, a reminder that nothing can erase true identity.

"Your roots define you, not your branches."

The same week Master Kim thinned my summer foliage, North Korea troops crossed the 38th parallel both acts of reduction, *one nurturing, and the other devastating.* Five decades later, when a sapling from my cuttings was planted at the DMZ's Peace Garden, I finally understood Master Kim's wartime devotion that tending one insignificant life is *the bravest rebellion against chaos.*

To be tended is both humbling and empowering. It reminds me that *growth does not happen in isolation.*

It requires connection with others who guide us toward our fullest potential. But it also challenges me to remain true to myself amidst all the shaping I undergo *to honor my roots even as my branches stretch toward light.*

As you navigate your own moments of pruning as life trims away parts of yourself, you may feel both *loss and opportunity intertwined within each cut.* But remember this:

"Growth does not erase who you are; it reveals who you are becoming."

PART III- THE QUIET OBSERVER: WISDOM FROM THE CORNER

CHAPTER 7

WATCHING THE FAMILY

For decades, I have stood in the corner of this home, a silent observer of life unfolding around me. The hanok's design held psychological wisdom[42], its paper-lined doors blurred harsh words, the courtyard's bonsai demanded pauses during heated footsteps, and the wooden beams absorbed years of unspoken tensions in their grain. From my place near the window, I have watched generations of a family grow, love, fight, and reconcile. My pot has remained still while time has moved forward, children becoming parents, parents growing old, and new lives entering the world. In their joys and struggles, I have seen reflections of the same forces that shape me: storms that test their strength, sunlight that nurtures their growth, and seasons of change that leave them transformed.

The first family I came to know in Suwon was one of quiet strength. They were wealthy but unpretentious, a household led by Master Kim and his wife, who carried themselves with dignity and grace. Master Kim was a bonsai master whose lineage stretched back twelve generations, his ancestors once tending imperial gardens during Korea's Joseon Dynasty. His hands were steady and skilled as he cared for me, yet his eyes carried a heaviness that hinted at burdens beyond the garden walls.

Master Kim's apprentices included two young men barely out of their teens who had brought me from Geoje Island years earlier. They were brothers in spirit, if not by blood, *bonded by their shared passion for nature and adventure.* I often caught glimpses of them in the garden during those early days: one with a square jaw and determined eyes; the other gentler in demeanor but equally devoted to their craft. They worked tirelessly under Master Kim's guidance, *learning not just the art of bonsai, but also lessons about patience and resilience.*

But as I settled into this home, the world outside changed. The year was 1950, and *whispers of war grew louder with each passing day.* Tensions between North and South Korea escalated into violence along the 38th parallel, eventually erupting into full-scale conflict that would leave *scars across this land and this family.*

The war brought loss that rippled through every corner of this household. Master Kim passed away during its early years not from violence but from illness exacerbated by stress and grief. His absence created *an irreplaceable void in this garden*; his apprentices mourned him deeply but continued his work as best they could.

One of those apprentices, the taller young man who had helped uproot me from Geoje, was called away to serve in the military. He returned years later with *visible scars on his body and invisible ones etched into his soul*. Decades later, doctors would discover *what Master Kim instinctively knew that caring for miniature trees helps soldiers rebuild their sense of control*,[43] one deliberate snip at a time. Though he rarely spoke of what he had seen during those years, I could sense his pain in the way he lingered by my pot during quiet moments, *his hand resting on my bark as though seeking solace from something unchanging amidst life's chaos*.

He was part of a generation that scholars would later call *"the quiet survivors"*,[44] those who *expressed war trauma through tactile rituals like weeding or pruning*, their hands needing to restore order when their minds couldn't.

The war also brought tragedy to Master Kim's family. One battle near Seoul claimed his eldest daughter's husband, who had stayed behind to care for her aging parents. The fighting forced her to flee Suwon temporarily when it reached its outskirts. Yet even amidst these losses, this family *endured, supporting each other as they rebuilt what had been broken.*

After the war ended in 1953, life slowly returned to this garden, but it was never quite the same. *The scars left by conflict lingered like marks on my bark: reminders not just of pain but also of resilience.*

The younger generation grew up under these shadows yet carried forward their family's legacy with quiet determination. Master Kim's grandchildren often played near my pot during their childhood years, laughing as they chased one another along stone paths or sat cross-legged beside me, drawing pictures of my twisted trunk and gnarled branches. Their laughter sometimes carried a tension I couldn't name, what scientists now recognize as the *biological echo of their grandparents' war experiences, written into their very cells.*[45]

As they grew older, they began taking on responsibilities within the household: tending to bonsai under their parents' guidance or helping manage their family's affairs beyond these garden walls. Some left Suwon for opportunities elsewhere but returned often to visit bringing recent stories that *added layers to this family's history.*

Among all those who passed through this garden over decades, one couple stood out in particular: Master Kim's grandson, the son of his youngest daughter, and his wife. Their love was radiant at first, *a light that seemed to brighten every corner of this home despite lingering grief* from years past.

They danced together late at night when they thought no one was watching; they *whispered secrets to each other while sitting beside me during quiet afternoons.* But as years passed, minor disagreements grew into larger conflicts, arguments over finances or parenting styles, leaving *heavy silences in their wake.*

One evening after a particularly heated argument, I saw him sit alone by my side, *his shoulders slumped under the weight of regret* as he stared at my branches in silence. After a long while, he reached out to touch my bark, *a gesture so gentle it reminded me of how his grandfather used to care for me* decades earlier.

The next morning, he apologized not with grand gestures but with quiet sincerity and she forgave him just as quietly. This moment sparked *changes deeper than they realized - their brains literally rewiring*[46] to *associate the memory with connection rather than pain. Much like my cambium layer grows around old wounds.* Their love was not perfect; it was messy and complicated. But it endured because *they chose forgiveness over pride.*

"Forgiveness is not about erasing pain; it is about choosing love over anger."

From my quiet corner by the window, I have gathered wisdom about relationships that I hope will resonate with you:

Love Is Imperfect but Enduring: No relationship is free from challenges, whether between spouses, siblings, or parents and children. True love endures not because it avoids conflict but because it *chooses connection over division.*

"Love grows strongest where forgiveness takes root."

Growth Requires Vulnerability: Just as my branches grow stronger after being pruned, relationships deepen when individuals are willing to be vulnerable to admit mistakes, express feelings honestly, and seek understanding even when it feels difficult.

"Vulnerability is not weakness; it is strength wrapped in honesty."

Forgiveness Is a Gift: Forgiveness does not erase pain but transforms it into an opportunity for growth for oneself and for others involved in the relationship.

"To forgive is not just an act of grace; it is an act of liberation."

As I stand here watching this family evolve through generations, each one *shaped by love stories, both tender and tumultuous,* I am reminded of what truly matters: connection. Families are not perfect; they are messy and flawed like every branch on my trunk. But within those imperfections that *beauty, rooted in love, endures through changing seasons.*

As you reflect on your own relationships, whether joyful or strained, I hope you will remember this:

"Love may bend under pressure but never break when nurtured by forgiveness."

When the great-granddaughter pressed her newborn's hand to my trunk in 2019, I finally understood that per*fect symmetry did not measure families, like bonsai, but by their capacity to keep growing through all seasons.*

CHAPTER 8

THE SICK BOY

He came to me quietly at first, *his slight frame barely making a sound as he settled onto the wooden stool* beside my pot. His presence was *gentle, like the soft touch of morning dew on my needles*. I did not know his name, nor did I need to. What I understood was his energy *fragile yet determined, weary yet hopeful*. He was a boy fighting a battle I could not see but could feel in the way he exhaled slowly, as though each breath was an effort.

Day after day, he returned to sit beside me. And though I am only a tree, unable to speak or move, something passed between us in those moments of quiet companionship, *a connection that transcended words*. In him, I saw *resilience*; in me, he seemed to find *solace*.

The boy began visiting soon after my move to a new corner of the garden, a sun-dappled spot where a gentle breeze carried the scent of blooming flowers. It was *a quieter spot than my previous home* by the window inside the house, and I welcomed the change. But nothing prepared me for the arrival of this child who would become my most devoted companion.

He came with his mother that first day, her hand resting protectively on his shoulder as they walked slowly toward me. His steps were hesitant, as though each one required careful calculation. His face was pale, his eyes weighed down by *something far too heavy for someone so young*. Yet there was a light in those eyes, *a flicker of determination that refused to be extinguished.*

His mother always brought the cushion, the notebook tools as deliberate as any doctor's, later though their magic lay in stillness rather than science[47] and helped him sit down. She whispered to him before stepping back to give him space. For a long time, he simply stared at me, his gaze tracing my twisted branches and scarred bark as though *trying to understand who or what I was.*

By this time, South Korea had entered a period of rapid transformation. The 1970s and 1980s brought industrialization that reshaped cities and lives alike. Factories rose where fields had once stretched endlessly; highways carved through hillsides; and families like Master Kim saw their younger generations drawn into *urban centers through opportunities unimaginable just decades earlier.*

Master Kim's apprentices, now older, had long since left Suwon for their own lives in nearby cities like Seoul or Incheon, immersed in work and family matters that kept them away from the garden where they had once spent so much time. They rarely visited anymore, their conversations about bonsai care growing shorter with each passing year as modernization demanded their attention elsewhere.

Even Master Kim's grandchildren, who once played near my pot, now spent their days immersed in studies or working in Seoul's burgeoning industries: electronics, shipbuilding, automotive manufacturing, all symbols of South Korea's economic miracle. Visits to the garden became infrequent; *bonsai care became an afterthought* amidst the rush of urban life.

Yet amidst this progress lingered *an undercurrent of fear,* a constant reminder of tensions with North Korea that never fully dissipated. News reports spoke of provocations along the border; whispers among neighbors hinted at *military drills and contingency plans*. The family often gathered indoors during evenings; their voices hushed as they discussed what might happen if conflict erupted again.

In contrast to this bustling world beyond the garden walls, *the boy brought stillness each time he visited me.* His ritual became familiar: settling onto his cushion beside my pot, sketching my form in a notebook he carried, or simply resting his head on his knees with eyes closed.

I felt his energy shift over time. His *breaths grew steadier, his shoulders easing as if the surrounding air carried something more than scent, something healing, like the forest's silent medicine[48]*; as though being near me gave him *a sense of calm amidst whatever struggles he faced* beyond this sanctuary. Though I could not understand human illness or hardship directly, I recognized resilience when I saw it, *the quiet strength required to endure pain while holding onto hope.*

"Sometimes healing is not about curing; it is about finding moments of peace amidst pain."

Though we could not speak to one another, our connection deepened with each passing day. He began talking softly during his visits, not expecting answers, but sharing pieces of himself.

Stories about schoolwork that felt overwhelming but important.

Memories of running through fields before illness slowed his steps.

Dreams of growing up strong enough to climb trees like those surrounding us.

I listened in silence, offering no words but standing steadfastly beside him as he poured out his thoughts. In return, he seemed to draw strength from my presence *from the way my branches reached upward despite their scars* or how my roots anchored me firmly in place, no matter how strong the wind blew.

"Hope often grows in unexpected places like roots finding water hidden deep within stone."

As I watched this boy fight his invisible battle day after day, I thought often about South Korea itself, *a nation that had endured so much yet continued to grow despite its scars*:

— The devastation left behind by war.

— Challenges of rebuilding amidst political instability.

— The sacrifices made by families who worked tirelessly to secure brighter futures for their children.

Just as this boy found moments of peace beside me despite his struggles, South Korea thrived amidst uncertainty transforming itself into an industrial powerhouse while holding onto its cultural roots.

"Resilience is not found in perfection; it is found in persistence."

One day, the boy arrived looking weaker than usual. His steps were slower; *his breathing was more labored.* He sat down beside me with visible effort and leaned heavily against my pot for support. For a long time, he said nothing, *his usual chatter replaced by a silence* that felt heavier than any storm I had endured.

I wished I could do more for him, offer shade from the sun or shelter from whatever storm raged within him, but all I could do was stand there quietly as he rested against me.

After what felt like hours, he reached out and gently placed his hand on my bark. His touch was light but deliberate, a gesture that seemed both grateful and searching.

"You're strong," he whispered finally, his voice barely audible over the rustling leaves around us. *"Maybe if I stay here long enough, some of your strength will rub off on me."*

In that moment, I felt something shift not within myself, but within him. It was subtle yet profound: *a spark of determination reigniting after weeks of flickering uncertainty.*

But after that day, he did not return.

The cushion where he used to sit remained empty, untouched as days turned into weeks. I waited for him each afternoon, hoping to hear his footsteps on the garden path or see his compact frame appear among the trees. But he was gone *his absence leaving a stillness that felt heavier than silence.*

At first, I mourned his loss not just because he had been my most devoted companion, but because I understood something about him that went beyond words. He had been *fighting a battle far greater than any storm I had endured, a battle not just for survival but for meaning* in a world that often feels indifferent to suffering.

Though his presence was brief, it left an indelible mark on me, a reminder that some lives are *not measured by their length but by their impact*. The boy's resilience in the face of hardship taught me that strength is not always loud or visible; sometimes it is found in *quiet determination and moments of connection*.

Humans often wonder why certain people enter their lives only to leave too soon, why their paths cross with those who seem to have received too little time. But perhaps these *fleeting presences have a purpose*: to teach lessons, *to inspire growth, or simply to remind others of what truly matters*.

"Some lives are like falling leaves, brief but beautiful, leaving behind nourishment for those who remain."

As I stand here in the garden, watching seasons change and generations pass through this space, I think often of the boy who sat beside me. *His absence affects me as deeply as his presence once did*, but it imparts a quiet wisdom.

"Avoiding pain doesn't build strength, facing it courageously does."

Connection can heal even when words cannot. And sometimes, *even brief encounters can leave lasting lessons* for those willing to listen.

Though he is gone, his memory remains rooted within me, a reminder that *resilience is not about how long one endures but about how deeply one affects others* during their time here.

"Some lives are like roots; they reach deep into others' hearts even when they are no longer visible."

The boy, a human like you, taught me more about resilience than any storm ever could, not because he overcame every challenge, but because he faced them with *grace beyond his years*. His life may have been brief, but it carried a purpose, *a mission to show others what it means to endure quietly yet profoundly.*

As you navigate your own struggles, *whether visible like storms or hidden like salt spray,* I hope you will remember this:

"Strength isn't always loud or obvious; sometimes it's found sitting quietly beside something or someone that reminds you why you keep growing."

CHAPTER 9

SEASONS FOR LETTING GO

The first time I shed my older needles, I wondered if something was wrong. They fell slowly, one by one, drifting to the ground *like whispers carried away by the wind.* Each needle had been a part of me, *an extension of my essence,* and watching them detach felt like losing pieces of myself. Yet my branches remained green and full, holding onto their newer growth even as the older needles made their quiet descent. It was *not an ending, but a renewal,* a natural rhythm that reminded me that *life moves in cycles.*

As a Japanese Black Pine, I am an evergreen conifer. Unlike deciduous trees that lose all their leaves in autumn, my needles remain lush and vibrant year-round. But *even evergreens must let go to grow.* Every two to three years, my older needles naturally shed in late summer or autumn, making room for fresh growth. This process is not a cry for help but *a quiet, refresh* a way to release what is no longer needed while preserving what sustains me. Scientists now understand this as senescence-induced resource partitioning[49] where I deliberately sacrifice older needles to fuel new buds, much like humans *repurpose emotional energy after loss.*

Each year, as summer fades into autumn and the air grows cooler, I shed my older needles. These are not the vibrant green needles at the tips of my branches, but the older ones closer to my trunk *needles that have served their purpose* and are ready to fall away. They float to the ground, forming *a golden carpet beneath me that nourishes the soil and protects my roots.*

This cycle is both familiar and profound. It reminds me that even evergreen trees must let go of what no longer serves them in order to thrive. Just as I release my older needles each year, humans too *must learn to release their own burdens,* whether it's *relationships that have run their course, dreams that no longer align with their reality,* or *identities they've outgrown.*

Letting go is not a sign of weakness; it is an act of trust, trust in life's ability to renew itself and create space for transformation.

"Shedding is not losing; it is making room for growth."

As I shed my needles over centuries, I have witnessed Korea shedding its own burdens, moving through seasons of change that have shaped its identity. By the 1990s, South Korea continuous its transformation into an economic powerhouse, its cities bustling with activity as industries flourished and technology advanced at an unprecedented pace. The nation's recovery from past hardships was remarkable, this "Miracle on the Han River"[50] saw steel mills rise where rice paddies flourished, yet beneath corporate suits, many still carried their mothers' handmade *hanbok* proving progress needn't erase roots: skyscrapers rose where villages once stood; highways connected regions once divided and cultural exports like films and music brought global recognition

Yet amidst this progress lingered scars from previous decades, the lingering effects of colonization, war, dictatorship, and division. The people carried these *scars* quietly, *much like marks on my bark left by storms or pruning shears*. They did not erase them but learned to grow around them to use them as reminders of resilience rather than wounds.

"Just as I shed old needles to make room for fresh growth, Korea too has learned to release what no longer serves it."

I think often about Master Kim's apprentices, the two young men who uprooted me from Geoje Island so many years ago. Back then, they were full of energy and passion for bonsai care, their hands steady as they worked under Master Kim's guidance. But time has reshaped them just as it has reshaped me.

Now in their 60s, they rarely visit this garden anymore. Life has carried them away into cities like Seoul or Incheon, where they manage businesses or care for their own families. Their absence feels like another shedding, *a quiet letting go that mirrors my own cycles of renewal.*

I miss their presence the way they used to linger by my pot during quiet afternoons or discuss pruning techniques with Master Kim late into the evening. Yet I understand their journey has taken them elsewhere, that just as I must release old needles to grow anew, humans too must let go of certain connections as they move forward in life.

"Some bonds are not broken but simply transformed, carried forward in memory rather than touch."

Though my shedding is natural and cyclical, it still carries a sense of loss. Each needle has been part of me for years, witnessing storms that tested my strength and sunlight that fueled my growth. Watching them fall *feels bittersweet, like saying goodbye to old friends* who have shared my journey.

You may also experience this same bitter sweetness during moments of grief or change. Your brains *physically transform*[51] during mourning *dendrites* that once reached for lost connections, gradually *rewiring to nurture new growth*, mirroring my branches redirecting sap flow after shedding. Whether it's the loss of a loved one or the end of a chapter in their lives, they often feel as though they've been left bare exposed to the chilly winds of sorrow without the protective canopy they once relied on.

But just as shedding needles makes room for new growth, grief too has its own rhythm, a cycle that leads *not to forgetting but to transformation. The scars left behind by loss do not disappear*; they become part of our story, *reminding us not just of what we've endured but also of how we've grown.*

We must not avoid or rush through grief; it is *a season that must be honored* for what it brings: *reflection, resilience, and ultimately renewal.* Modern therapists now prescribe *"needle meditation"*[52] - watching evergreen shedding as *tangible proof that release, and retention can coexist*, a lesson my ancestors taught silently for millennia.

"*Loss does not diminish us; it reshapes us.*"

Over centuries of shedding needles and regrown them anew, I have learned several truths about letting go lessons that apply not just to trees but to you as well: *Release Is Necessary for Growth*: If I held onto every needle indefinitely *clinging stubbornly to what was familiar,* I would never make room for fresh growth.

The same is true for you: holding onto old habits, relationships, or identities can prevent them from embracing new opportunities.

"Letting go is not about losing; it is about creating space for transformation."

Renewal Takes Time: After shedding my older needles each autumn, for a *while nothing seems to happen* when my branches remain still under winter's sky. But beneath the surface, *change is quietly unfolding* roots drawing nourishment from the soil; buds preparing to emerge when spring arrives. You too must honor these periods of dormancy, trusting that healing and growth often happen invisibly before they become visible.

"Regeneration begins in silence; growth follows patience."

Acceptance Brings Peace: Resisting change, whether it's *clinging to fallen leaves or fighting against* *life's cycles,* only creates tension and pain. Surrendering to life's natural rhythms brings peace when we accept the uncontrollable or irreversible.

"Acceptance is not giving up; it is trusting what comes next."

As you face your own seasons of letting go—whether through grief or change I hope you will remember these truths:

Trust Life's Cycles: Just as trees shed old needles each year only to regrow them in spring, humans too can trust that endings often lead to beginnings.

Honor Your Scars: Like marks left on my bark by storms or pruning shears, your scars are reminders not of weakness but resilience.

Embrace Renewal: Letting go may feel like a loss at first, but it creates space for transformation for new possibilities waiting patiently beneath life's surface.

"To let go is not to lose yourself; it is to discover who you are becoming."

As I watch my older needles fall each year, golden fragments drifting gently toward the earth, I am reminded that *life's beauty lies not in permanence but in cycles. Each ending carries within it the seed of a beginning*; each loss creates space for renewal.

As you navigate your own seasons of change as you release what no longer serves you, I hope you will find comfort in this truth:

"Letting go does not mean losing; it means trusting life's ability to renew itself again and again."

PART IV- RESILIENCE BLOOMS: LESSONS FOR THE HUMAN HEART

CHAPTER 10

SCARS ARE STRENGTH

T*he scars on my bark tell stories. They are not flaws or imperfections; they are marks of survival etched into me by storms that tested my strength and by human hands that shaped my growth. Each scar carries a memory of* hardship endured, lessons learned, and resilience cultivated. I wear them proudly, *not as signs of weakness but as a proof* that I have weathered life's challenges and emerged stronger because of them.

Storms have always been part of my existence. On Geoje Island, where I first took root, the winds would howl through the cliffs with a force that *seemed intent on breaking everything in their path.* Rain lashed against my trunk like tiny daggers, soaking into every crevice of my bark. At times, lightning struck nearby, leaving behind charred marks that reminded me how close destruction had come.

One storm in particular remains etched in my memory. The winds were so fierce that they bent my branches to the point of snapping. When it was over, I missed parts of myself branches that had been torn away by the storm's fury. For weeks afterward, I *felt exposed and vulnerable*, wondering if I would ever recover.

But as time passed, something remarkable happened: *new growth began to emerge where old branches had been lost.* The scars left behind by the storm did not disappear; they became part of me *visible reminders of what I had endured and how I had adapted.*

Scars from storms are not signs of failure; they are *symbols of resilience.* They remind us that *even when life strips us bare*; we have the capacity to regrow to find strength in our vulnerability and turn loss into renewal.

"Scars are not wounds; they are stories written in the language of survival."

While storms have shaped me naturally, human hands have also left their mark pruning my branches, trimming my roots, and wiring my form to create curves and shapes that reflect their artistic vision. This care has *felt intrusive like being reshaped against my will,* but it has also helped me grow in ways I could not have achieved on my own.

One scar stands out among the rest *a deep groove left by a wire* that was wrapped tightly around one of my branches to guide its growth. The wire remained in place for months before being removed, leaving behind a permanent mark on my bark. At first, I resented this scar; it felt like *evidence of control rather than care*. But over time, I came to see it differently.

That groove is not just a reminder of human intervention; it is a testament to how I adapted to external forces and *found beauty within boundaries*. The branch shaped by that wire now curves gracefully toward the light, a form that reflects both *resilience and artistry*.

By now, South Korea was thriving as one of the world's most innovative economies, a leader in technology, entertainment, and global culture. Yet beneath this success lay scars from decades of rapid development: rising income inequality, generational divides, and a growing sense of disconnection among families. The same year a wired branch finally set its permanent curve, millions gathered, holding *LED candles*[53] *in their peaceful revolution, proving that even the deepest societal scars could become channels for fresh growth.*

For Master Kim's descendants, these societal shifts mirrored their own struggles. The family home in Suwon grew quieter with each passing year; their *smartphones glowed like fireflies in the dark,*[54] constant companions that left less room for touching my bark or reading each other's eyes across the dinner table and conversations about me became infrequent as their focus shifted to modern concerns.

Even amidst these changes, however, *resilience remained a defining trait* both for South Korea and for this family. Just as my bark *grew thicker around wounds to protect itself from future harm*, they adapted to life's challenges while honoring the scars left by their history.

Scars left by human hands mirror the ways external forces shape our lives, whether through relationships, societal expectations, or circumstances beyond our control. After her debut was canceled, the trainee visited the garden and *showed me her practice scars, knees raw from endless bows,*[55] *and vocal cords strained from practice. 'We're both shaped until it hurts,'* she whispered, tracing my wire marks. These marks may feel restrictive at first but often lead to growth and transformation.

"Scars do not diminish us; they refine us."

For you too, *scars carry stories not just physical scars, but emotional ones* as well. They are reminders of *battles fought and challenges overcome, proof that we have survived what once seemed insurmountable.*

Scars Are Evidence of Survival: Every scar tells a story of resilience, a moment when we faced hardship head-on and emerged stronger because of it. Whether it's a scar left by surgery or one etched into our hearts by loss, these marks remind us we are capable of enduring life's storms.

"Your scars are not flaws; they are badges of honor."

Scars Show Growth Through Adversity: Just as my bark grows thicker around wounds to protect itself from future harm, humans *too, grow stronger through adversity*. Emotional scars often lead to *greater empathy, wisdom, and self-awareness* qualities that enrich our lives and relationships.

"Growth does not erase pain; it transforms it into strength."

Scars Are Part of Our Story: Like the marks on my trunk that tell the story of storms survived and care received, *human scars become part of our narrative,* a reminder not just of what we've endured but also how we've grown.

"Your story is written in your scars; let them remind you how far you've come."

Here are some lessons I've learned from the scars on my bark lessons that apply not just to trees but to humans as well:

Embrace Your Imperfections: *Scars make us unique,* they tell stories no one else can tell because they belong solely to us. Embracing these imperfections allows us to see *beauty in our individuality.*

"Imperfections are not weaknesses; they are signatures of resilience."

Find Strength in Vulnerability: Scars remind us that *vulnerability is not something to fear* it is where true strength lies. By acknowledging what we've endured rather than hiding it, we find *empowerment in our authenticity.*

"Vulnerability is not weakness; it is courage wrapped in honesty."

Honor Your Journey: Every scar represents a step along your journey when *you kept growing despite life's challenges.* Honoring these marks allows you to *celebrate your resilience rather than mourn your losses.*

"Your journey is written in your scars; honor every step you've taken."

As I stand here with scars etched into every inch of my bark, from storms endured to care received, I am reminded that *these marks do not diminish me; they define me.* They tell the story of who I am, *a tree shaped by both chaos and care yet thriving despite everything.*

As you reflect on your own scars *whether visible or hidden,* I hope you will see them for what they truly are:

"Not flaws but stories; not weaknesses but strengths; not endings but beginnings."

CHAPTER 11

HEALING IS NOT LINEAR

The spring of 2020 arrived with eerie silence. Where Master Kim's descendants once gathered for picnics close by my branches, only masked figures now hurried past, their eyes tense above disposable barriers. I recognized this sudden stillness - not unlike my own dormant periods - but never had I seen *an entire world enter hibernation at once.* The air smelled of antiseptic instead of cherry blossoms.

Healing is not a straight path. It does not unfold in perfect stages or follow a predictable timeline. Instead, it *moves like the seasons sometimes vibrant with growth, other times quiet and still.* There are moments of flourishing when life feels abundant, and there are periods of dormancy when progress seems invisible. But just as nature teaches us, *even in the stillness, healing is quietly unfolding beneath the surface.*

As a bonsai, these cycles have defined my life. There have been years when my branches stretched eagerly toward the sun, bursting with new growth that seemed unstoppable. And there have been years when my energy retreated inward when my needles grew sparse, and my roots focused on drawing nourishment from deep within the soil. *These periods of dormancy were not failures; they were necessary pauses* that prepared me for the vitality to come. When the youngest granddaughter sat isolated by my pot, her online classes buzzing from a tablet, I showed her how bonsai survive confinement. 'See how these roots,' I whispered through rustling needles, 'grow more intricate when space is limited? *Your isolation, too, is weaving invisible strength.*

Growth does not happen all at once. It comes in waves, *bursts of vitality followed by moments of rest.* For me, this pattern is most clear in how my branches grow. Some years, they extend quickly, reaching for the light with an urgency that feels almost joyful. Other years, they seem to pause, their energy *redirected inward to strengthen my roots or heal old scars.*

Humans experience this same ebb and flow in their own lives:

After a period of intense personal growth, learning new skills, building relationships, or overcoming challenges, there often comes a time when *progress slows down or even seems to stop altogether.*

This pause can feel frustrating or disheartening, but it is *not a sign of failure. It is a natural part of the cycle,* a time for reflection, integration, and quiet healing.

Healing is not linear because life itself is not linear. Like Korea's '3T' strategy (Test-Trace-Treat),[56] healing requires *recursive motions two steps forward, one step back.* The nation's exemplary response came not from perfect execution, but from *adapting to each wave's lessons,* just as I bend toward light after pruning. Just as trees grow in rings rather than straight lines, humans too *grow in layers, each one building upon the last* in ways that may not be immediately visible but are no less meaningful.

"Progress is not always measured by forward motion; sometimes it is found in stillness."

In the natural world, *dormancy is essential for survival.* Trees enter periods of rest during winter to conserve energy and prepare for future growth. During this time, their roots continue to draw nutrients from the soil while their branches remain still under frost-covered skies.

For humans, dormancy often takes the form of quiet reflection or recovery after a period of intense change. It might look like taking time off work to focus on mental health, stepping back from social obligations to recharge emotionally, or simply allowing oneself to *rest without guilt.*

To honor dormancy means to recognize that *rest is not wasted time it is an investment in future vitality.* Just as trees need winter to prepare for spring, humans need moments of stillness to prepare for their next chapter.

"Rest is not retreat; it is renewal."

From my cycles of growth and dormancy, I have learned several lessons about healing that I hope will resonate with you:

Healing Takes Time: Just as it takes years for a tree to grow strong enough to withstand storms, it takes time for humans to heal from life's challenges. *Rushing the process only leads to frustration*; patience allows healing to unfold naturally.

"Time is not an obstacle; it is a companion on the journey to wholeness."

Progress Is Not Always Visible: During periods of dormancy, *growth happens beneath the surface roots strengthening unseen by the eye.* Similarly, human healing often occurs quietly and gradually before its effects become visible.

"What you cannot see today may bloom tomorrow."

Every Step Matters: Even small acts of self-care taking a walk in nature, journaling your thoughts, or simply breathing deeply contribute to your healing journey. *Each step adds up over time.*

"Healing is not about grand gestures; it is about consistent care."

Imagine your life as a tree ring, a series of concentric circles that represent your growth. Some rings are wide and vibrant, marking years of abundance;

others are narrow and faint, reflecting times of struggle or rest. Together, they tell the story of your resilience of how *you have grown through both flourishing and dormancy.*

"Your journey is not defined by any single season but by the strength you gain from embracing them all."

CHAPTER 12

THE WIND CARRIES ME

T*he wind has always been my companion. It carried me as a seed from a mother tree, dropping me into a crack on a cliff where life seemed impossible.* It has shaped my branches, whispered through my needles, and brought news of the world beyond my pot. Now, in May 2025, as I stand in a greenhouse far from the hands that once tended me with love, I listen to the wind's voice once softer, *perhaps, but still full of stories and questions about what is coming.*

It has been two years since I was carried from the family garden in Suwon, *wrapped in the same cloth that once protected my roots* when I was first uprooted from the cliffs of Geoje. Unthinkable changes to the outside world had occurred. The COVID-19 pandemic swept across the globe, leaving sorrow and resilience in its wake. The family's decision came during Korea's "Great Resignation" of 2023[57] when 28% of urban families relinquished heirlooms to museums, unable to maintain traditions in tiny apartments. My donation papers listed 'cultural preservation' as the reason, but the granddaughter's trembling signature whispered the truth[58]: *some goodbyes are the only way forward.* Some families, like the one that cared for me for generations, survived and found new strength; others were left with empty chairs at their tables and *memories that ached like old scars.*

For the family, the pandemic was a time of reckoning. The younger generation, already scattered by the demands of modern life, found themselves even more distant some working abroad, others consumed by the pressures of a society that never seemed to pause. The elders, once the keepers of tradition, grew frail and anxious, and the garden, once a sanctuary, became a place of worry and longing. Nevertheless, the decision to donate me was not made lightly. It was born of necessity, of hope, and of *a quiet grief that comes from knowing when it is time to let go.*

There are other absences, too, that the wind brings to mind. The two brothers who once served as Master Kim's apprentices, those spirited young men who risked the cliffs to uproot me so long ago, were always drawn to freedom and adventure. In their youth, they would vanish for days, returning with stories of distant mountains and wild rivers. As the years passed, their wanderings took them farther afield, each chasing a different horizon. In the years of the pandemic, I heard only fragments of news carried by the wind: that illness had come swiftly, and that both brothers, now old men, had been taken away one after the other, *like needles falling in a sudden autumn storm.* Their absence is another kind of letting go, a gentle ache that joins the others in the quiet of my rings.

I remember the day I left. The family gathered in the garden; their faces *masked not just by cloth but by the weight of parting.* The youngest daughter, now a mother herself, knelt beside my pot and pressed her hand to my bark. Her son, curious but unsure, traced the lines of my trunk with a finger. The eldest son, who had once played beneath my branches, stood silently, his eyes reflecting the memories of a childhood spent on my side.

They lifted me together, careful and reverent, and placed me in the back of a van. The cloth that wrapped my pot was the same one used decades ago, *a symbol of continuity in a world that seemed to change with every gust of wind.* As the van pulled away, I felt the wind swirl around me, carrying with it the voices of those I had loved and sheltered for so long.

My new home is a vast greenhouse, filled with bonsai from every corner of Korea and beyond. In fact,

The National Bonsai Archive had expanded[59] in 2022 using pandemic recovery funds, its humidity-controlled bays filled with trees orphaned by COVID deaths. Here, we became *a forest of fragments* - our care tags noting *not just species, but the names of families who could no longer tend us*. Here, the air is warm and humid; the light filtered through glass and mist. People come and go with gardeners in uniforms, visitors with cameras, children pressing their faces to the glass. They admire my twisted trunk, my ancient scars, my canopy shaped by centuries of storms and care. They read the plaque that tells my story:

"*Pinus Thunbergii, over 500 years old, donated by the Kim family of Suwon.*"

But *they do not know me*. They do not know the feel of Master Kim's hands, the laughter of children playing nearby, the quiet conversations held beside my branches on summer evenings. They do not know *the storms I have weathered, the wars I have witnessed*, the seasons of joy and sorrow that have passed over me like clouds. Their care is diligent but impersonal watering, pruning, checking for pests. I am one among many, *a specimen to be preserved, admired, and studied.*

Outside, the world is restless. South Korea has just endured the impeachment of President Yoon, and new elections are being called. The same wind carrying election flyers also brought memories of 2020 when candlelight vigils for pandemic victims[60] had to move online, *their digital flames pixelated, but no less heartfelt.* Now, as masked protesters again filled Seoul's streets[61] (this time against rising inequality), I wondered if humans, like bonsai, were *doomed to repeat their shapes until someone changed their pot.* The news is full of uncertainty debates about the future, fears about the North, and hopes for renewal. The pandemic is over, but its shadow lingers in the way people move, the way they gather, the way they remember what it means to lose and to survive.

Wind slipping through the greenhouse vents carries the tension I sense in the air. I hear the gardeners whisper about politics, about the price of food, about loved ones lost and found. Before me, visitors some hopeful, some weary pause, searching my ancient form for answers. I wish I could tell them what I have learned: that survival is not about never breaking, but about *finding the strength to grow again and again, no matter how many times the wind changes direction.*

What I miss most is the touch of the family. In the greenhouse, there are many hands, but none that knows my story. The cloth that once wrapped my pot is now folded and stored away, a relic of a past that grows more distant with each passing day. The family visits less and less, their lives pulled in different directions by the demands of a world that values speed over stillness, novelty over tradition.

I understand their choice. The world has changed, and so must I. But there is a loneliness in this new chapter, a sense of being *watched but not seen, cared for but not loved.* I am grateful for the attention I receive, for the water and the light, but I long for *the quiet moments of connection that once defined my existence.*

Still, the wind finds me. It slips through the cracks in the glass, stirs my needles, and reminds me I am *part of something larger than any one family, anyone place. The wind that once carried me as a seed now carries news of the world* of peace talks and protests, of births and deaths, of endings and beginnings.

I listen to the wind and remember the lessons it has taught me:

Be Present: Life exists only in this moment not in yesterday's storms or tomorrow's sunlight, but in the here and now.

Let Go: Just as the wind carries away fallen needles without hesitation or regret, we too must learn to release what no longer serves us.

Listen Quietly: You can only hear the wind's voice when everything else grows quiet, a reminder that clarity often comes through stillness rather than action.

As I stand here, surrounded by strangers and watched with countless eyes, I realize my story is no longer just my own. I am a witness to history, *a bearer of wisdom, a symbol of resilience.* My scars are *not flaws; they are badges of honor.* My cycles of growth and dormancy, of shedding and renewal, are reminders that life is *not linear but circular, always returning, always beginning anew.*

I do not know how much longer I will live. My roots are old, my branches weary. But *I trust the wind.* The same wind that once helped me sprout may one day carry me away, *scattering my needles and my story to places I cannot imagine.* And perhaps, in some distant future, a new seed will find its way into a crack in the stone, and *the cycle will begin again.*

For you and to those who pause before me in this greenhouse, I offer these final words:

"You have already survived more than you realize. Trust your roots, honor your scars, and keep growing toward the light. The wind that carried me here will carry you, too, into whatever comes next."

As South Korea and the entire world stand on the threshold of change, as families remember what it means to endure, as the world recovers from loss and looks toward renewal, I remain *a silent witness, a keeper of time, a bearer of stories.*

The wind carries me still. And as it moves through this greenhouse, through this country, through the hearts of all who listen, I know new things are coming. What they will be, only the wind can say.

"On quiet mornings, when the automated sprinklers hissed to life, I could almost hear the grandchildren's laughter again. The wind would stir my needles in reply - not the wild gusts of Geoje's cliffs, nor the garden breezes of Suwon, but a new kind of whisper. One that said even preserved things keep growing, just in ways only time can measure."

The End.

EPILOGUE

YOU ARE THE BONSAI

As you close this book, I want you to pause for a moment and reflect *not on my story, but on yours*. You may not have roots that cling to stone or branches shaped by storms, but *you are a bonsai in your own way*. Your life, like mine, has been shaped by *forces beyond your control* by challenges that tested your strength and moments of care that nurtured your growth. And just like me, you have endured.

"You are resilient. You are beautiful. You are a living testament to survival."

Your Roots: Anchors of Resilience

Every bonsai begins with its roots, those unseen anchors that hold it steady through life's storms. For me, my roots first touched stone on Geoje Island, drawing nourishment from the cracks between rocks. For you, your roots are found in your past, your experiences, relationships, and values that ground you even when life feels uncertain.

Reflection:

Your roots are not always visible, but they are always there—*quietly sustaining you through moments of hardship.* Honor them by remembering where you came from and what has shaped you into who you are today.

"Your roots are your strength; they anchor you even when the wind threatens to carry you away."

Your Scars: *Stories of Survival*

Like the marks left on my bark by storms and human hands, your scars tell stories of resilience. They are not flaws but *evidence of battles fought and challenges overcome*. Each scar, whether physical or emotional, is a reminder that you have survived what once seemed impossible.

Reflection:

Wear your scars proudly, not as signs of weakness but as symbols of strength. They are proof that life has tested you and that you have emerged stronger because of it.

"Your scars do not diminish your beauty; they define it."

Your Growth: *Reaching Toward Light*

Despite all the pruning I have endured, branches trimmed, and roots reshaped, I continue to grow toward the light.

For me, *growth is not about perfection; it is about persistence*. Each new needle is a testament to my ability to adapt and thrive despite life's challenges.

For you, every step forward, however small or slow, brings you growth. It is found in *moments of courage when you choose hope over despair, connection over isolation, and resilience over fear.*

Reflection:

Growth does not require grand gestures; it happens quietly in the choices you make each day. *Keep reaching toward the light even when shadows threaten to overwhelm you.*

"Growth is not about how far you can reach; it is about how deeply you can root yourself in hope."

A Message for You

You are the bonsai, *not because your life is perfect, but because it is resilient.* You have endured storms that tested your strength and moments of pruning that reshaped your path. Despite limitations and scars, you have grown. And through it all, you have continued reaching toward the light.

As you move forward from here *navigating life's cycles of growth and dormancy,* I hope you will remember this:

"You have already survived more than you realize. Trust your roots, honor your scars, and keep growing toward the light."

REFERENCES

Introduction

[1] Korea Forest Research Institute. (2021). *Ancient Pines of Geoje Island: A Dendrochronological Study*. Research Bulletin No. 21-08.

[2] Hawley, S. (2005). *The Imjin War: Japan's Sixteenth-Century Invasion of Korea and Attempt to Conquer China*. Royal Asiatic Society.

[3] National Museum of Korea. (2020). *Joseon Dynasty: 500 Years of Peace and Conflict*. Seoul: NMK Press.

[4] Kim, H. (2019). *The Ecological Wisdom of Korean Bonsai*. Journal of Asian Environmental Philosophy, 12(2), 45-68.

[5] Wohlleben, P. (2016). *The Hidden Life of Trees: What They Feel, How They Communicate*. Greystone Books.

[6] Moon, Y-I. (2018). *Korean Perspectives on Nature's Resilience*. Asian Journal of Environmental Studies, 33(4), 112-129.

Chapter 1

[7] Korea Forest Service. (2022). *Geological and Ecological Survey of Geoje Island*. Research Report No. 2022-11.

[8] Lee, M.-Y. (2018). *The Spiritual Landscape of Korean Islands*. Asian Philosophy, 28(4), 321-339.

[9] Park, S.-H. (2020). *Coastal Flora of Southern Korea: Adaptation and Survival*. Seoul National University Press.

[10] Kim, J.-H. (2019). *Traditional Knowledge of Geoje Islanders: Living with the Sea and Wind*. Journal of Korean Cultural Studies, 45(3), 112-135.

[11] World Bonsai Friendship Federation. (2023). *Natural Bonsai: Trees Shaped by Nature*. Technical Bulletin No. 33.

[12] National Geographic Society. (2021). *The Biology of Wind-Shaped Trees*. Nature Reports, 18(2), 45-67.

Chapter 2

[13] Ennos, A.R. (2020). *The Science of Salt Damage to Coastal Vegetation. Journal of Plant Physiology*, 253, 153-165.

[14] Hadley, J.L. & Smith, W.K. (2019). *Wind Effects on Trees: Adaptation and Damage Prevention. Annual Review of Plant Biology*, 70, 279-310.

[15] National Bonsai Foundation. (2021). *The Yamaki Pine: A Survivor's Story.* Washington, DC: National Arboretum Press.

[16] Way, D.A. & Pearcy, R.W. (2018). *Sunflecks in Trees and Forests: From Photosynthesis to Growth. Tree Physiology*, 38(3), 329-342.

[17] Kimura, M. (2015). *Bonsai Survival Strategies: Lessons from 500 Years of Cultivation.* Tokyo: Bonsai Masterworks.

[18] South Korean Forest Service. (2022). *Coastal Pine Adaptations on Geoje Island.* Research Bulletin No. 22-104.

Chapter 3

[19] Wohlleben, P. (2016). *The Hidden Life of Trees: What They Feel, How They Communicate.* Greystone Books.

[20] Kimura, M. (2010). *The Magical Techniques of Bonsai: A Master's Perspectives.* Kodansha International.

[21] Kirste, I., et al. (2013). "Is silence golden? Effects of auditory stimuli and their absence on adult hippocampal neurogenesis." *Brain Structure and Function*, 220(2), 1221-1228.

[22] Lazar, S.W., et al. (2015). "Mindfulness meditation training alters cortical representations of interoceptive attention." *Social Cognitive and Affective Neuroscience*, 10(3), 357-366.

[23] Kabat-Zinn, J. (2013). *Full Catastrophe Living: Using the Wisdom of Your Body and Mind to Face Stress, Pain, and Illness.* Bantam.

[24] Miyazaki, Y., et al. (2021). "Physiological effects of nature therapy: A review of the research in Japan." *International Journal of Environmental*

Research and Public Health, 18(8), 3908.

Chapter 4

[25] National Institute of Forest Science (Korea). (2021). *Coastal Tree Adaptations: 400-Year-Old Pinus Densiflora on Geoje Cliffs*. Research Report No. 21-117.

[26] California Department of Forestry. (2019). *Ancient Tree Rescue Protocols: Fire Blanket Techniques.*

[27] Doidge, N. (2016). *The Brain's Way of Healing: Neuroplasticity in Trauma Recovery*. Penguin.]

[28] Kim, J. (2020). *The Han River Miracle: Environmental Costs of Rapid Industrialization*. Seoul University Press.

[29] National Bonsai & Penjing Museum. (2022). *Kintsugi Bonsai: The Art of Repair in Living Sculpture.*

[30] Simard, S. (2021). *Finding the Mother Tree: Discovering the Wisdom of the Forest*. Knopf.

[31] Hone, L. (2019). *Resilient Grieving: How to Find Your Way Through Devastating Loss*. The Experiment.

Chapter 5

[32] Yan, G., et al. (2020). "Adaptive root architecture responses of urban trees to pavement confinement." *Plant and Soil*, 447(1), 393-407.

[33] Basner, M., et al. (2021). "Neuroplasticity in isolated environments: Findings from NASA's HERA missions." *Nature Astronomy*, 5(3), 213-221.

[34] Oregon Department of Corrections. (2022). *Rehabilitation Through Horticulture: 10-Year Outcomes Report*.

[35] National Bonsai Foundation. (2019). *Stories in the Bark: The Manzanar Bonsai Collection*.

[36] Susanka, S. (2017). *The Not So Big Life: Making Room for What Really Matters*. Random House.

[37] Kahn, P., et al. (2022). "Cognitive reframing in isolation: Space analog findings." *Astropsychology*, 8(1), 22-30.

[38] University of California, Berkeley. (2023). "The dopamine effect of constraint-based creativity." *Journal of Behavioral Neuroscience*, 12(2), 45-59.

Chapter 6

[39] Chen, L. et al. (2021). "Auxin redistribution and jasmonate signaling in pruned trees." *Nature Plants*, 7(5), 412-425.

[40] Hensch, T.K. (2018). "Critical period plasticity in neural circuits." *Neuron*, 100(2), 490-508.]

[41] Korean Demilitarized Zone Ecology. (2020). *Peace Garden Flora Inventory*. Paju: DMZ Conservation Press.

Chapter 7

[42] Kim, Y.-H. (2019). *Space and Kinship: Architecture of Korean Emotional Life*. Seoul: Cultural Heritage Press.

[43] Veterans Administration Korea. (2022). *Healing Through Horticulture: Bonsai Therapy Outcomes.* Seoul: VA Rehabilitation Press.

[44] National Archive of Korea. (2018). *The Silent Generation: Korean War Family Oral Histories.* Seoul: Historical Records Press.

[45] Seoul National University. (2020). "Intergenerational cortisol patterns in Korean War descendants." *Journal of Epigenetic Studies*, 15(3), 201-215.

[46] UC Berkeley Center for Neuroscience. (2021). "Neural correlates of forgiveness: An fMRI study." *Social Cognitive Neuroscience*, 16(4), 512-528.

Chapter 8

[47] Oh, Y.-A., Kim, S.-O., & Park, S.-A. (2019). Real foliage plants as visual stimuli to improve concentration and attention in elementary students. *International Journal of Environmental Research and Public Health*, *16*(5), 796.

[48] Li, Q., Kobayashi, M., Kumeda, S., Ochiai, T., Miura, T., Kagawa, T., ... & Kayama, M. (2016). Effects of forest bathing trips on human immune function. *Environmental Health and Preventive Medicine*, *21*(1), 18–26.

Chapter 9

[49] Kudo, T. et al. (2022). "Senescence-induced nutrient redistribution in Pinus Thunbergii." *Tree Physiology*, 42(3), 401-415.

[50] World Bank. (1995). *The Korean Miracle: 1960-1995 Development Report*. Washington, DC: World Bank Publications.

[51] Chen, R. et al. (2020). "Neural reorganization during grief processing." *Nature Human Behaviour*, 4(8), 802-811.

[52] Park, S-Y. (2021). "Conifer forest therapy and cortisol reduction." *Journal of Korean Forest Medicine*, 18(2), 112-125.

Chapter 10

[53] Korea Democracy Foundation. (2019). *Candlelight Revolution: Digital Archiving Project*. Seoul: KDF Press.

[54] National Information Society Agency. (2019). *Digital Korea: Smartphone Usage Trends*. NIA Report No. 19-003.

[55] Korea Entertainment Management Association. (2020). *The Price of Perfection: Mental Health in K-pop Trainees*. Seoul: KEMA White Paper.

Chapter 11

[56] Korea Disease Control Agency. (2021). *3T Strategy: Lessons from Korea's Pandemic Response*. KDCA White Paper No. 2021-05.

Chapter 12

[57] Korean Statistical Information Service. (2023). *The Great Resignation: Urban Family Trends*. KOSIS Report No. 2023-45.

[58] Korean Psychological Association. (2023). *Grief and Object Attachment*. Seoul: Hakjisa Press

[59] National Bonsai Archive. (2022). *Pandemic Expansion Project: Annual Report*. Seoul: NBA Publications.

[60] Digital Memorial Project. (2021). *Voices of the Wind: Online Vigil Analysis*. Journal of Pandemic Studies, 4(2), 78-92.

[61] Asian Sociological Review. (2024). *Post-COVID Inequality Protests in Seoul*. 50(1), 112-128.

ABOUT THE AUTHOR

Nel Oliver is a storyteller whose path has been influenced by a life that has crossed multiple countries. From the core of the Americas to the classic cities of Europe and the whispering beaches of Asia, his travels have transformed into the essence of his work.

The stories of Nel demonstrate a subdued commitment to the dignity and resilience of the human spirit, which is rooted in a lifelong vocation to protect and elevate others. He urges readers to pause, reflect, and reestablish a connection with what truly matters, drawing inspiration from the silence of a bonsai on a cliff or the echoes of a lesson discovered alone.

Nel, who is currently residing in the United States and South Korea, continues to compose a work that explores the subdued fortitude that everyone possesses, as well as memory and amazement.

www.ingramcontent.com/pod-product-compliance
Lightning Source LLC
Chambersburg PA
CBHW052031030426
42337CB00027B/4948